Reconoce tus emociones/
Know Your Emotions

ENOJO ES ...
ANGRY IS ...

por/by Connie Colwell Miller

CAPSTONE PRESS
a capstone imprint

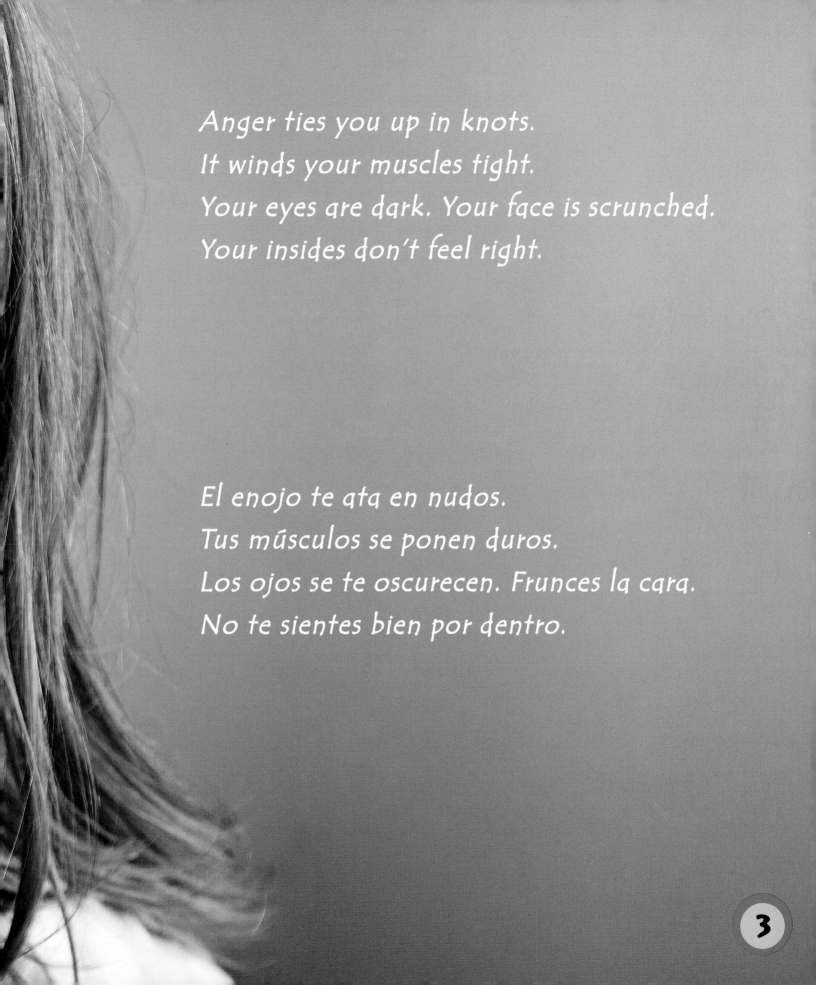

Anger ties you up in knots.
It winds your muscles tight.
Your eyes are dark. Your face is scrunched.
Your insides don't feel right.

El enojo te ata en nudos.
Tus músculos se ponen duros.
Los ojos se te oscurecen. Frunces la cara.
No te sientes bien por dentro.

3

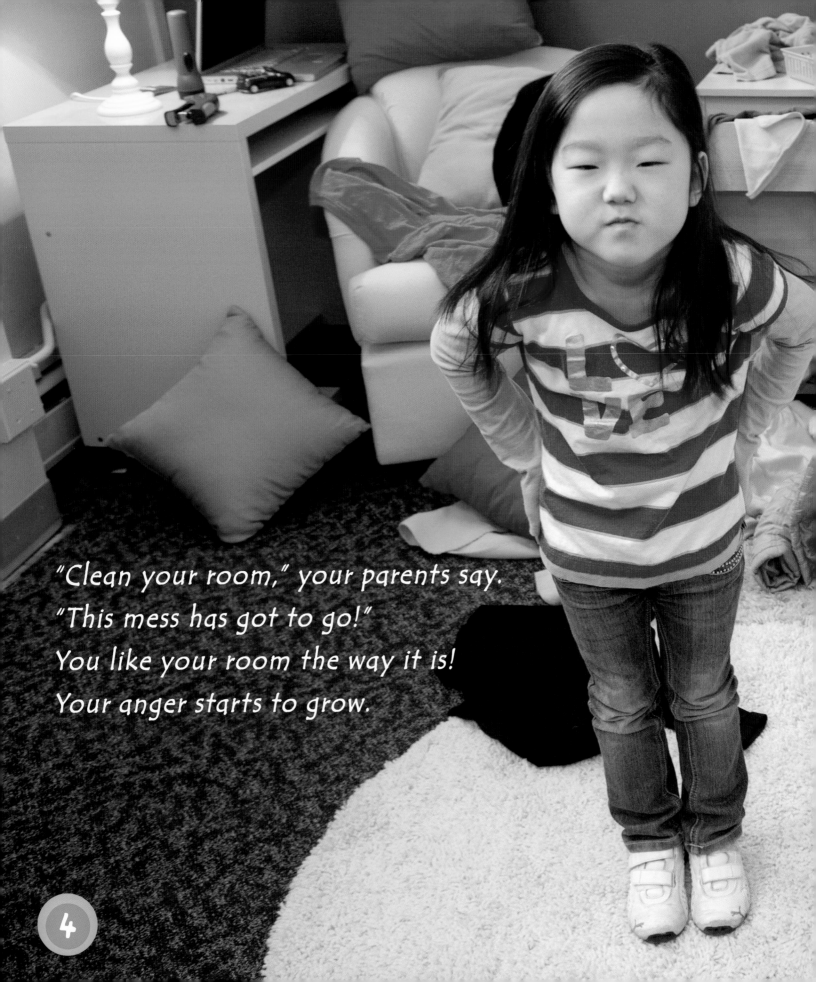

"Clean your room," your parents say.
"This mess has got to go!"
You like your room the way it is!
Your anger starts to grow.

4

"Limpia tu cuarto", te dicen tus padres.
"¡Este desorden debe irse!"
¡Tu cuarto te gusta tal como está!
Tu enojo comienza aumentar.

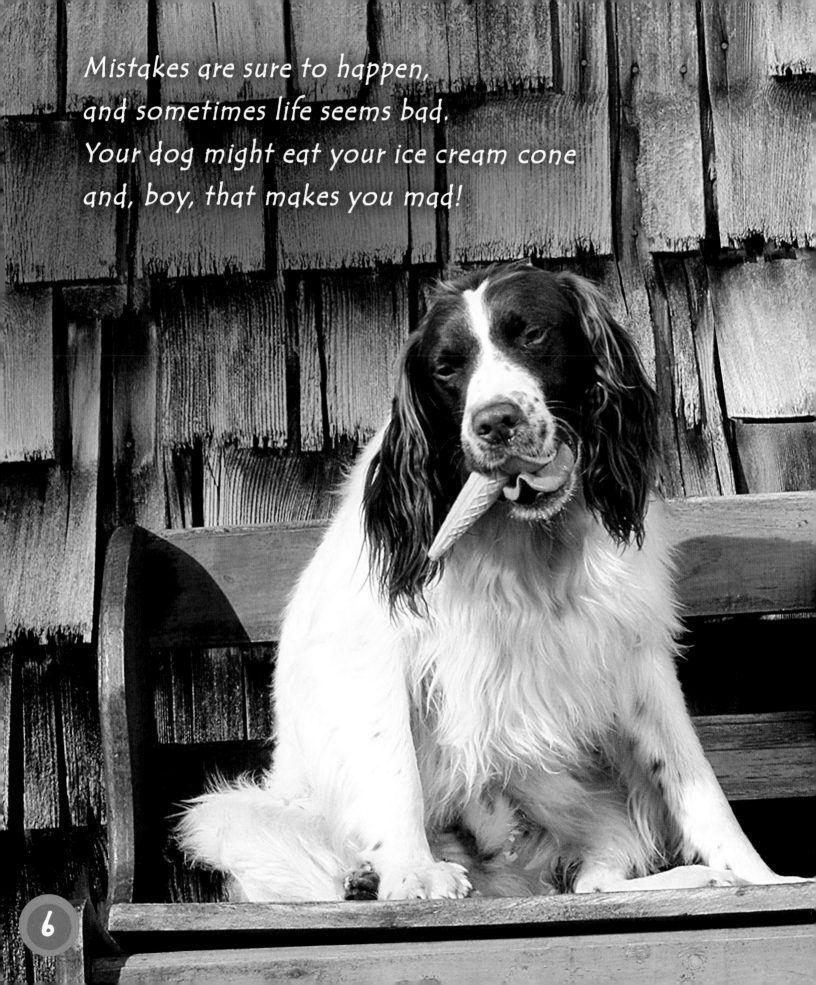

Mistakes are sure to happen,
and sometimes life seems bad.
Your dog might eat your ice cream cone
and, boy, that makes you mad!

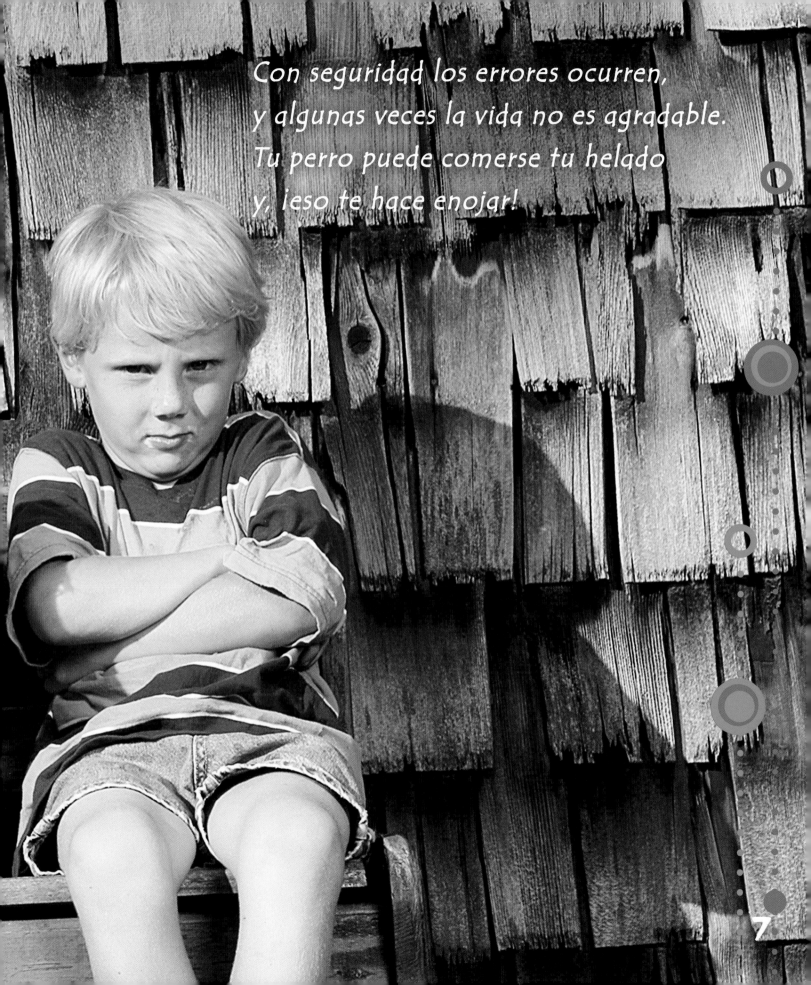

Con seguridad los errores ocurren,
y algunas veces la vida no es agradable.
Tu perro puede comerse tu helado
y, ¡eso te hace enojar!

7

You let a friend play with your toy.
She broke it right in two.
Anger fills you up inside,
and you're not sure what to do.

Dejas que una amiga juegue con tu juguete.
Ella lo rompió a la mitad.
Tu enojo empieza a aumentar
y no sabes qué hacer.

You just can't stand steamed broccoli!
It never tasted great.
You want to shout and stomp your feet
when mom says, "Clean your plate!"

¡No toleras el brócoli al vapor!
Nunca ha tenido un buen gusto.
Quieres gritar y patalear
cuando Mamá te dice, "¡Limpia tu plato!"

Oops! It slipped—a no-no word
you didn't mean to say.
You felt bad, but now you're mad—
you're grounded for the day!

12

¡Ay! Se te escapó una mala palabra
que no quisiste decir.
Te sientes mal, pero ahora estás enojado
porque estás en penitencia por todo el día.

13

On the couch, you get so mad—
your brother makes a face.
He sits too close. He bothers you.
He won't give you your space!

En el sofá, te enojas mucho
porque tu hermano te hace burla.
Se sienta muy cerca. Te molesta.
¡Él no te da espacio!

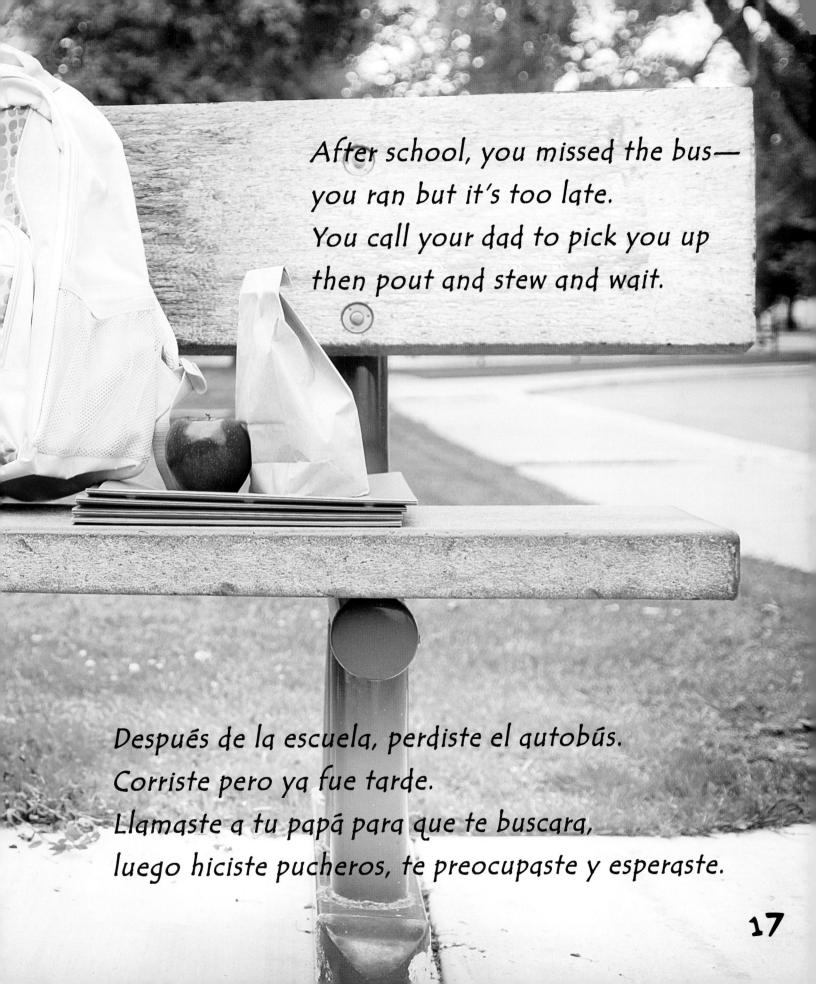

After school, you missed the bus—
you ran but it's too late.
You call your dad to pick you up
then pout and stew and wait.

Después de la escuela, perdiste el autobús.
Corriste pero ya fue tarde.
Llamaste a tu papá para que te buscara,
luego hiciste pucheros, te preocupaste y esperaste.

Anger's racing in your mind—
you need to let it out.
Find a place where it is safe
to scream or cry or shout.

El enojo corre por tu mente
y necesitas liberarlo.
Encuentra un lugar seguro
donde puedas chillar, llorar
o gritar.

It's true we all get mad sometimes.
We feel it now and then.
But when it grows, just let it go—
you'll feel like you again!

Es verdad que todos nos enojamos a
veces. Lo sentimos de vez en cuando.
Pero cuando es demasiado, déjalo
irse . . . ¡Te sentirás como tú mismo
otra vez!

Glossary

ground—to punish someone by not allowing them to leave

pout—to push out your lips when you are angry or disappointed about something

race—to run or move very fast

scrunch—to squish together

Internet Sites

FactHound offers a safe, fun way to find Internet sites related to this book. All of the sites on FactHound have been researched by our staff.

Here's all you do:

Visit *www.facthound.com*

Type in this code: 9781620651544

 Super-cool stuff! Check out projects, games and lots more at
www.capstonekids.com

Glosario

correr—hacer algo con rapidez

fruncir—arrugarse en señal de enojo

la penitencia—castigar a alguien al no permitir que se vayan

el puchero—empujar hacia fuera los labios cuando uno está enojado o desilusionado sobre algo

Sitios de Internet

FactHound brinda una forma segura y divertida de encontrar sitios de Internet relacionados con este libro. Todos los sitios en FactHound han sido investigados por nuestro personal.

Esto es todo lo que tienes que hacer:

Visita *www.facthound.com*

Ingresa este código: 9781620651544

 ¡Algo súper divertido! Hay proyectos, juegos y mucho más en www.capstonekids.com

A+ Books are published by Capstone Press,
1710 Roe Crest Drive, North Mankato, Minnesota 56003
www.capstonepub.com

Library of Congress Cataloging-in-Publication Data
Miller, Connie Colwell, 1976-
[Angry is—. Spanish & English]
Enojo es— = Angry is— / por Connie Colwell Miller.
p. cm.—(A+ bilingüe. Reconoce tus emociones = A+ bilingual. Know your emotions)
ISBN 978-1-62065-154-4 (library binding)
ISBN 978-1-4765-1088-0 (ebook PDF)
1. Anger in children—Juvenile literature. 2. Anger—Juvenile literature.
3. Emotions in children—Juvenile literature. I. Title. II. Title: Angry is—.
BF723.A4M5518 2013
152.4'7—dc23   2012017054

Summary: Simple text and photographs describe how it feels to be angry—in both English and Spanish

Credits
Jeni Wittrock, editor; Strictly Spanish, translation services; Alison Thiele, designer; Eric Manske, bilingual book designer; Svetlana Zhurkin, media researcher; Jennifer Walker, production specialist; Sarah Schuette, photo stylist; Marcy Morin; studio scheduler

Photo Credits
Capstone Studio/Karon Dubke, 1, 4–5, 8–9, 12–13, 14–15, 20–21
iStockphoto/Bonnie Jacobs, 10–11; Chris Fertnig, 6–7; Leigh Schindler, cover; Rosemarie Gearhart, 16–17
Shutterstock/Benjamin Haas, 18–19; JPagetRFphotos, 2–3

Note to Parents, Teachers, and Librarians
This Reconoce tus emociones/Know Your Emotions book uses full color photographs and a nonfiction format to introduce the concept of being angry. *Angry Is …* is designed to be read aloud to a pre-reader or to be read independently by an early reader. Photographs help listeners and early readers understand the text and concepts discussed. The book encourages further learning by including the following sections: Glossary, Internet Sites, Index. Early readers may need assistance using these features.

Printed in the United States of America in North Mankato, Minnesota.
082019   002560

INDEX

ÍNDICE